Feck o

"A concise guide to help you win back control"

Paul Bunce

Copyright ©Paul Bunce, 2018. All rights reserved.

ISBN: 9781728767697

Cover design by Paul Bunce

Copy and editorial assistance by Chris Bunce

Disclaimer:

I am not in any way medically trained, so please bear with me if you experience a less than professional medicinal approach; however, I really want to get my ideas out there, so that some readers can benefit from our shared investment of time, me by writing my experiences in this guide and you by reading them. The overriding difficulty is to fashion a guide into a succinct guide that is both easy to follow and useful for future reference, I hope that this format is acceptable to you and that I have reduced any needless clutter, whilst at the same time being understanding of your illness.

It must be emphasised that this guide on its own is not to be recommended as a fix for serious bouts of depression- I suggest that you seek out and engage with medical professionals as well, remember that you are the expert about yourself and what you may need on your road to recovery- I wish you luck on your journey.

Dedicated to:

You on your journey.

Table of Contents

DISCLAIMER:	3
INTRODUCTION:	6
LET'S LOOK AT IT ANOTHER WAY	8
WHO THE FECK IS BORIS!	15
INSIDE	18
FOOD	20
OUTSIDE	22
RELATIONSHIPS AND FAMILY	25
THE W WORD! (WORK)	29
NEW EXPERIENCES	32
WHAT ABOUT A RELAPSE?	36
DID I MENTION EXERCISE?	40
TIME TO RECHARGE	44
HOW TO USE YOUR TOOL KIT/SKILLS?	47
NORMAL SERVICE WILL NOT BE RESUMED	49
THE FUTURE	51

Introduction:

This is a guide to help long or short term sufferers of depression whatever the cause, with some strategies that I have used in a variety of circumstances. Some succeeded, whilst others had little effect and others helped to lift me from the glum murky smog, albeit briefly in some cases.

This is not from a medical practitioner's viewpoint, more of an experienced lifelong patient of depression and how I try to understand and deal with it. I decided to write a concise guide about these coping strategies as I have reached a time in my life that I feel strong enough to undertake such a challenge. I also believe that by not sharing these ideas to others would be a wasted opportunity, as I would like others to also benefit.

Depression is a proper crappy illness, one cannot "snap out of it" or "man up" as much as the sufferer would like to be able to, it can also be a symptom of something else that has decided to make your life shitty. In my situation, this has been from a mixture of bipolar disorder and borderline personality disorder coupled with trauma experienced as an ex-boarding school pupil.

Either way the cause can be from many aspects of rich sounding medical problems that are either hard wired into us from birth or have been accumulated throughout our lives by dealing and surviving horrible and vicious experiences, all might I add were beyond our control.

So, the most important thing to take from this guide is that your cause of depression whatever it may be was not in any way your fault; you did not invite it to inject itself into your life. Where we do have the power to change is how we respond and equip ourselves to limit the damage that it is trying to cause in our day to day lives. These methods are as individual as our personalities and I am sure that you already have some experiences of some small wins; we now need to capitalise on these and arm ourselves for our future happiness and resilience.

Let's look at it another way

Yes, I have experienced and continue to experience depression, even after 53 years applying many strategies to help me cope. What I am now able to experience is a more reduced version of it, a less deliberating and destructive influence than before. I think that this is in part by my approach and recognition to its ever-present strong authority and it is this power of control that I want to impart to you.

You need to understand that it always has the potential to rise-up and bring you down, this depression wants to ruin your happy times and extend and deepen your sad times. Recognise that it is there as an uninvited guest to your private house party and treat it as such, with contempt and absolute rejection that it deserves. This will start to put this dark monster into a place that has less power, less prominence, less significance and less influence. We shall now refer to this uninvited guest as "**Boris**"; no one wants a Boris in their life, time to start dissing him. Boris is bad for us, feck off Boris!

You have lived with Boris's crass influence for too long, he has been part of your emotional responses to the world around you, it is now time to separate, he has been allowed to ruin too much of your life already. The sad times became more melancholy and the limited happy times have been restricted, like a blocked funnel flowing slower and slower until the experience of being happy has become a distant memory. Feeling guilty when you should be happy forces you into having a skewed emotional response, which after a while does become your normal self, no wonder you are confused and exhausted.

So how did this all start? I truthfully am not in a position to answer that, you know the cause or causes, they are personal only to you, however I do know about the resultant outcome with the opening curtain that introduces Boris. The feelings that have been experienced are not dissimilar to what most people have felt, the intensity and its duration do become unique to the individual, which is strong, dark and foreboding.

Let's try to be positive for a while, what you have experienced so far has put you in places that many people will hopefully never experience, proving that you are a fighter that has been to a horrible place and returned, a reluctant tourist that has survived, richer in experience and stronger in personality.

You need to recognise that this power is intensely concentrated and if it could be bottled and sold it would make Olympians of us all. However, in its current form it is stunting your development and even hurting you, which is quite frankly disgusting for anyone to have to withstand in their lives. I will not even disrespect you by discussing the levels of Boris that can be experienced, you already know that and do not need me to remind you.

This is a guide for self-help strategies looking forwards, there is no benefit looking at what has been unless that's your particular avenue of resolution-it's up to you. I wish to concentrate on the future which, being unwritten is where you have full and total control over, you just need to seize it.

There are many medical models that can be discussed on how different strategies may be used, I personally hate that idea as it attempts to box us in, to being text book creatures that must respond in a precise manner. If we don't react as planned, then have we failed? The solution can only be discovered, nurtured and grown by you, as it must have your own identity, it will be a part of you in the same way as Boris is. I hope to set you on a path that makes your mind open to methods to keep Boris at bay, behind a virtual electric fence if that helps, it's up to you, you deserve to take back control of your life and enjoy its journey through both highs and not so low, lows! The demanding emotional drain of a Boris being either currently present or on the distant horizon is extreme and unsustainable, you are not superhuman, although you may think you are sometimes!

Remember back to when Boris was ineffective in your life and remained only a small dark feeling that was easier to subdue and push away? Well remembering that time may help as you had more control of your emotions then. Or recall when you started to feel its power start to engulf and take over your existence.

These moments are now to be part of your new tool kit as emotional strength weapons, use them wisely as they are powerful. If you do not have or cannot remember a time that you were fully in control of your emotions, don't fret as you are still placed to feel the powerful dominance of the negative thoughts, feel that as power and mentally construct an anti-Boris weapon, place it securely in your tool kit.

Let's use our mind to create a solution; after all, it will make a refreshing change to be in control again.

We will keep re-visiting our growing tool box throughout the guide, don't misplace it, that's the tool box not the guide! Where you are now emotionally is important for the guide to work, as you need to be able to direct and use some mental agility, to break free for a while in your mind, to have emotional resources at your disposal. If you are weak currently, then wait for a while, just plant the seed in your mind, feeling it nourish as time passes, you will know when you are stronger.

Accept who you are, as a unique individual that has had a rough time so far, yes there are parts that we all want to be; better, smaller, thinner, taller, longer, the list goes on, however, we will beat Boris with our mind, that is what we need to tune up. So, let's concentrate on that for now, start to name your depression with a name of your choice, I choose Boris but please feel free to call it whatever you want, at the end of the day it is personal only to you.

Choose a name and at the same time associate it with a character of a weak, scrawny and lethargic sad excuse of a thing, it will be the most pitied object you have ever known. Out of interest my Boris is a slimy reptilian creature that is both feeble and frail, you don't want it around and you would certainly not introduce it to your mates. You may currently see your version of Boris as too strong and controlling even taking the above into account but as time goes by you will be able to rebuff this view and shrink its influence.

Let's recap, you now have in your mind store a tool kit, containing a strong emotional weapon, you have identified and named your beast and dressed it with a less than favorable identity. Keep working on these as they can evolve using just the incredible power of imagination that we all have.

Who the feck is Boris!

Your depression is yours and yours alone, no one person apart from you can understand its ferocity and what it is like to live with on a day by day basis. The medical profession understands the biological reactions that take place but I found that of little comfort, I can feel it and by the same token detest its emergence.

Anti-depressants do provide some important help so always be accepting to these aids as it will help you to regain some important strength and control for the battle ahead. I assume that as you are reading this guide you or someone you know has been living with a Boris in their life. To have to withstand the constant low mood as it ebbs and flows like a tidal sludge pool is arduous.

Some try to hide it from their friends and families as if it is some sort of virus and try to battle through, others do not wish or are unable to hide its presence and respond by changing their behavior and become withdrawn and live a life akin to being in a coma. Nothing positive can ever be insinuated about Boris and its arrival, lives are never the same after its visit, if you have not sought medical advice and it has started to bite in your life then now is the time to do so, take it from me, it is part of the recovery process.

With your mood low and enjoyment being a thing of the past, the determination that you had may be seriously reduced, you need to start making some small wins and soon. I suggest that the quickest and easiest (I was concerned calling it easy, as I know better, nothing is easy when Boris is around) small win is order in your life. Having order means setting out a daily routine and sticking to it, so be practical and set a routine that has a greater chance of succeeding, even if it is just a small change. If it feels more orderly to you then that is sufficient, it can always be amended and updated later when you feel like it. Write it down, put it on the wall, tell everyone in the house that that is your daily routine, if they have any problems then it's time to discuss it, if you are up to it, if not I am sure that they can read and digest it for themselves-you are the focus now. Your routine should include rough timings as well, trying to include the three important new additions, soon to be added to your daily routine:

1. Inside
2. Food
3. Outside

Inside

This is our safe-haven in a storm, it is warm, comfortable and familiar and we surround ourselves with reminders of our lives in here. But when Boris is bad these reminders take on an alter ego and remind us of what we are missing, as if the good times are slipping through our weak, wet fingers. It is inside that we need to make a sanctuary, it is in here that we will start to win our battles, we need to associate and link our physical inside, be it a house, flat or caravan with our mental inside. Although I know that it is inside that we have the long sleepless nights, the destructive and hurtful arguments and the staying in bed for eternity.

It's this inside that may be operating theatre clean or as messy as a 2 year olds toy box, it does not matter; these are not priorities, look around and feel safe with yourself. Consider how much sleep you are currently getting, ask yourself is it too much or far too little, is it interrupted, if so do you know why? Write this information down somewhere so you can refer to it when designing your routine. You can be yourself here and be who you want; it's your refuge and retreat.

The inside is your default position, this is where you will be found when the following two items are not in play, consider what you will be doing inside. Jot down some ideas on your routine. Avoid just sitting in front of the telly watching dull and uninspiring programs, either turn over to a documentary or turn it off. I believe that looking out of a window is far more interesting than enduring the majority of the rubbish on the goggle-box. You have clearly found reading, so propel your interests into fields that interest you.

Food

Some people that are experiencing Boris will eat too much and others far too little, or a combination of both at different times. Your body is the powerhouse for your mind and remember it is the mind that we want to strengthen to combat Boris. Therefore, it seems that fulfilling our appetite correctly with healthy foods is the way forward. Take-away food provides calories I will agree but does little to sustain our bodies in a healthy long term program. We need to educate ourselves by listening to our bodies and feeding it accordingly, this is not a cook book so I will not insult you with recipes-just eat well and include some fruit as well. Obviously, the body needs to be nourished and as strong as possible, again small changes at first. After you have given it some thought include rough times and details of the food that you will have on that day's routine.

Outside

This is both a place of wonder and a place of fear and anxiety, with a Boris waiting behind most corners. The outside needs to be tackled carefully, not too soon, not too much and where possible in areas that you know. It is here that we are tested as we come across strangers that make many assumptions upon us, such as "he looks miserable" or "why does she look scruffy?"

You need to ignore and reject these assumptions, unless they are in your safe circle of friends and family you do not owe them anything. I will keep coming back to it but the most important person in this equation is you, remember, You! You can join in their small talk when you are able to, until then look after yourself.

The most important aspect of the outside for you is to walk whilst getting valuable exercise, as in your tool kit you want to invest in some sort of regular exercise. This does not have to be a marathon a day, just a short walk in all weathers, this is what you need to start producing some of your brains most powerful hormones. I have found personally that exercise is better than anything to shunt the brains feel good hormones, giving an additional strength to battle Boris. If you detest walking then consider some other form of exercise, either on your own or in groups- its once again completely up to you. If you have regular exercise in your tool kit, it will be the most potent arsenal available to you and I speak from experience. In your growing daily routine, it is time to add the outside details of where, when and what.

You now have more tools for your tool box, still take it steady and do not be disappointed if you hit a relapse, learn from the bad times and try again when ready. Do not rush change as it will need to gain a firm foothold if it is to be a benefit to the long term. Put your routine in a prominent place and read through it, understand and absorb its contents, decide on who you wish to share it with and finally congratulate yourself for another victory.

Relationships and family

The relationships in your life I hope are valuable and nurturing, possibly a little strained as well at times thanks to Boris (not you), these relationships should also be positive experiences as well. What if they are not? Well only you know how you feel about a solution but perhaps not right now if you are really under the influence of Boris. Avoid any major decisions until Boris has left the building.

I also hope that your close relationships are understanding about your illness and are aware that you are struggling through as best you can, given the circumstances. Your friends are lucky people as they have found you, the very person that is honest and frank and dishes out advice to others. However, I am sure that during bad times you are a recluse and are as difficult to find as Lord Lucan riding Shergar! It is well known detail that it tends to be the kindest people that get shackled with a Boris, remember this fact, as you probably have a poor self-esteem image of yourself, thanks to the twisted feelings when visiting the dark pits of despair. For every relationship, no matter the type, it is all dependent on one important person and that is you, if you are feeling fragile and exposed then of course you will not be at your best and suspicious at worse.

Your relationship experiences will improve as you start to banish the negative feelings from your life, you should then be able to identify any toxic relationships that are not good for you. Families obviously have different ties to you and are muddied by concepts of duty and responsibility, either way these need to be on equal terms to you as an adult in your own right.

One method to help understand your close family and friends is to write their names down on a piece of paper and identify how these individuals are part of your life and what positive and negative influence they have on you. From that you can see who is your supporter when needed and who depends on you for support. This will then allow you to understand the role that your own relationships of all types can help you during your battle with Boris. Confide in your close relationships that you are battling an illness, if they do not already know; it is surprising how much additional help can be provided by people that already have a personal insight.

This sharing might also alleviate some of the pressure that may be present on a close relationship, then you are heading towards you goal, as part of a team. Other supportive relationships that are proven to help you are that of a suitable support group. You may shudder when I mention this as if you are like me the possibility of being in a support group fills me with dread. However, I have been to a few and after my initial hesitations it turned out that they are not dens of despair, quite the opposite. Only you will know if you are feeling strong enough to attend one of these, if not now, you can still investigate what is available in your local area so that it is ready when you are fit to ascend that step.

The W word! (Work)

"Work is a constant struggle without an illness, what chance have I got"? or "Will I be able to hold my job down due to my illness"? These are some of the constant questions I asked myself whilst at work. When I was well I was a very effective part of a working team but when ill I was a letdown, quite frankly, or so I thought. Turns out that most of the time I exaggerated in my mind what was happening.

I fell foul of Boris and my working expectations changed from being totally realistic to ultra-sensitive akin to self-loathing. So, what can I glean from coming out the other side of this maelstrom? Well firstly you work to live and not live to work and as we are not robots we will sometimes become ill and breakdown. The workplace can sometimes be instrumental in making any illness worse by the practices they employ, so I suggest that if you feel work is not helping you much that you discuss this with your GP, manager, union representative, Occupational Health, work colleagues in fact anyone that can help. I know that we want to soldier on through thick and thin but that is for comic book heroes, not us. Statistics tell us that 25% of the population will have a mental health issue at some point so it is highly likely that you are not alone in work fighting a Boris. Additionally, under the Health and Safety at Work Act 1974 your workplace has a duty of care over you whilst you are at work, which translated means that all work places must assess the amount of stress and other negative influences that you could be exposed to.

So, work should not be an additional source of anxiety, it should be supportive and understanding. Talking about your situation to the relevant person/department should aid you and may be an area of additional support on your journey to better health. I found that when in work and feeling very low I had trouble prioritising work that had to be done that day, tomorrow or next week, also I forgot important deadlines which all combined together to make me feel next to useless. Then I found a solution which was a simple small notebook that I kept in my pocket and I would jot down tasks that I had to do with deadlines and other important duties that were needed, at the same time a desk diary helped me to organise chores in a timely manner.

Try these methods as remembering things when Boris is about is like trying to herd cats, it is virtually impossible.

New experiences

The ability to respond to new experiences is made so much more difficult to nigh on impossible when feeling low. There is just no enthusiasm to try new things, better to stick with what we know restricting ourselves to exposure to items new. This is such a shame as to restrict oneself to new experiences is throttling back our ability to learn new skills. So what is the solution to this dilemma? Well again, this depends on the current state of mind and your determination.

The adage of "feel the fear and do it anyway" may be pertinent here but again concentrate on just small wins only. To try new things even when you are feeling anxious is painful but this is where the secret lies, treat it as a challenge. A challenge can be anything that pushes your boundaries, makes you feel on edge, requires you to dig deep.

I will share one of my examples with you which although extreme does give some strategies that can be employed along the way. I was new to teaching and although I had taken many classes in a further education college I was tasked to take the entire year group for one and half hours in a lecture theatre that had a capacity of 100 students. On top of that all the departmental teaching staff would also be present. I was dreading this especially as the subject of health and safety is not always inspiring or enthralling for a 17-year-old. This was going to be a tough crowd.

A few days before the typical emotions reared up, the first was avoidance; could I get out of this gig? I did consider if this was possible and then I asked myself, why was I dreading doing my job, why would a lecture to more students and staff make me feel so scared? Boris was now on the horizon, what could I do? If I avoided delivering the lecture Boris would still strike, if I did the lecture would that keep Boris at bay? So many questions filled with doubt, then the next emotion came to a head, being absolute frozen terror.

I was stuck between a rock and a hard place; it seemed as if I was going to suffer either way. Then I was lucky to have an epiphany, I would turn it into a challenge. Just changing its label to a "challenge", changed my approach to it overnight. I felt invigorated; I would also try to incorporate new teaching strategies with more student involvement, in addition to multi-media snippets to reinforce learning objectives. This swift transition from something that was going to hurt me regardless, to inspiring my creative juices was instrumental in other life experiences. The lecture went very well which helped to seal the deal. But if it went poorly that would not matter as the challenge was accepted, its outcome becomes another agenda.

So, if you find yourself in a situation that makes you feel uncomfortable just take a moment to re-adjust your objectives into a new challenge. You will surprise yourself on what you thought you could not achieve and experience new and exciting things.

You can change its name from a challenge if you wish, to anything that you prefer, such as, task, trial or test.

What about a relapse?

Trying new things and approaching situations in a different manner will not always go according to plan. It is important not to be disheartened when this occurs as it is part of the changes that you are investing in. If something goes wrong, try to consider what went wrong and why, replay it in your mind and see if it was indeed as bad as you first thought, how did you feel before and now afterwards?

Remember how you feel immediately after a poor experience will always slightly dissipate a while afterwards, so analyse it only when you feel strong enough to do so. These visits into unsafe emotional areas although uncomfortable can help to strengthen your resolve, so next time you would have built up a natural resistance.

So, it has gone wrong and you feel worse than before, perhaps you are vulnerable and sensitive to all around you, before hiding away, ask yourself the following, what did you want to happen? Sometimes our expectations are too high or sometimes other people's expectations of us are also elevated. Try to discover what you wanted to happen and what would have been a more acceptable outcome. This reflection will use your minds power to answer the questions thus deflecting Boris's power. You have also started to create a template of what would have been more acceptable.

Even with the world going according to plan there is always a possibility and sometimes a probability that you will have a relapse and Boris takes over again, resulting in a worsening condition to your mood and enthusiasm. You understand its impact personally and know its strength, however, within that maelstrom during small periods of rebellion, consider what you have achieved so far. You have not failed; you have encountered an opportunity of deliberation which after its dominance is reduced, will allow you to continue stronger.

Don't give up trying as every time you will move closer to keeping the power and control that you deserve.

Do you have a support mechanism in place? Friends and/or family members that can support and help you to understand the situation you have encountered is invaluable in the recovery process. One fall out effect of having a relapse is the creation of avoidance techniques, you were burnt before so why try or do that again?

This is a natural human process as we do not go out of our way to become ill and will find a path of least resistance to dodge the devastating feelings that a relapse represents. That is why it is crucial that you unwind what has happened for the relapse to happen in the first place, was it trying too much, too soon or being well out of your comfort zone. This scrutiny of the occurrence will help you to learn and evaluate its triggers, with a view to mentally remembering to lessen the next incident. What should be in your mind is that with a healthy understanding the next relapse may be avoided or lessened-listen to yourself and your investigations. Finally, in this point when you reflect, was the relapse a suitable outcome to what happened? or was it excessive? was it real or perceived danger? Knowing this information will equip you better, as remember information is power.

Did I mention exercise?

Yes, I know that I have covered this before but it is so important it deserves a chapter on its own. One of the reasons I am writing this guide is to share my own experiences and techniques that I used to lessen Boris's grip on my life. I put a lot of that down to exercise and the benefit it has on your minds health.

A stronger mind is less prone to certain illnesses as it gives more strength to your thought process, you can liken it to a link between our physical and mental self. Do not for one minute think I am asking you to become superhuman, I am not, just to consider doing some form of exercise that you may not currently do now.

This exercise can take the form of individual activities such as cycling, walking, running, swimming, going to a gym or in a team activity covering all the previous and includes activities such as tennis, badminton, dancing, yoga etc. the list is endless. Your local leisure centre will be a brilliant source of information, as will any local support groups. If you are new to exercise then make sure that you have your doctor's support before starting, you want to getter better not worse. This way any concerns of your physical readiness can be evaluated and considered.

When you do start be cautious, as at the beginning the release of natural positive feeling hormones called endorphins will be a welcome surprise. These are not illegal and it is your bodies' way of saying thank-you. Try not to get too hooked on these as you may find yourself going from little to no exercise to extreme amounts, as you become addicted to its effect. This happened to me and I ended up cycling hundreds of miles a week, Boris was quelled during the rides but my physical body was knackered! it was unsustainable. Strive for balance.

Once you have started your chosen exercise try to add this to your daily routine, how often do you do this? This again is your choice but the experts do say that around 30 minutes a day is the most therapeutic. There should also be next to no cost in pursuing your choice of exercise, again your local leisure centre may have special deals where you can attend outside their main busy times, so you may get a discounted deal.

Exercise must be a pleasure for you and not a chore, if after a while it still feels unpleasant then look for another type of exercise, there are many types out there. Also, give it time, as the benefits will not be felt overnight, they tend to creep up on you slowly but will become part of you after a while. I suggest once you have found the exercise that you like give it 2-3 months for it to really sink into your life. Sometimes trying to find time is difficult, so a good plan of your routine should allow you to shoe-horn in some valuable activities.

"But I can't be arsed to do exercise, give me other solution!" I hear some of you say. I was once in the same situation looking for methods to fight my illness and I did not believe that exercise would do it for me. I was wrong, exercise made a major impact in my life, it took time and still continues to do so but I also know the alternative is too hideous to contemplate. Once you feel the link between your mind and your body and its positive authority you are on a progressive and upbeat path.

Get your heart racing, feel the power within and recognise its time for you to start feeling in control of your life.

As *Confucius* said:

- *"a thousand mile journey begins with one step"*

- *"It does not matter how slowly you go as long as you do not stop"*

Time to recharge

You mind has gone through a lot so far and only really gets some down time when you are asleep, not just a few minutes' nap here and there, as that is insufficient, it demands full on deep sleep for between 6-8 hours, no more and no less. My own experience of sleep is that it is a refuge during bad times, I had far too much of it and I always felt drained of energy and life.

This I do not need to tell you is not healthy and sets a breeding ground for Boris and its manifestation. Poor sleep hygiene is against our instincts, we are designed to sleep overnight and not during the day (unless you have trained it by working shifts), it is important that you clean up this act as soon as possible. The lethargic feeling needs to be banished and soon.

The only way is to teach yourself good sleep patterns and set that into a routine. If you just lie there trying to sleep and your mind just wanders and doesn't tire then welcome to the club, mine also does the same. I mentioned exercise earlier, that can be a conduit for better sleep as even if the mind is fully awake the tired body will demand sleep. Listening to quiet music can sometimes help, a bath before bed is also apparently a good one to aid relaxation.

Work on what works for you, it will be trial and error for a time until something fits. You may even find that medical intervention from your GP in the form of sleeping drafts may help, just try to avoid being zonked out during the day. Being in the modern world and using technology may help as there are plenty of apps for phones that have sleep monitoring software for free.

Whatever you try, you are aiming to adjust your sleep pattern into a regular routine. This will free up energy to be used during your waking hours.

How to use your tool kit/skills?

Here is a recap of your tool box and your newly focused skills:

- Historic emotional dominance over Boris.
- A visualised, silly parody of your version of a Boris-it is embarrassed and weaker as a result.
- Your own exercise routine with the power it provides.
- A growing organised life reflected in your daily written routine.
- Better balance of sleep, food and relaxation.

You have come a long way in just over 45 pages-well done.

These skills that you have been developing will assist you in your goal of subduing your Boris. So, if a situation arises take comfort and strength from the weapons that you have created and fashioned from your own experiences and knowledge.

This is also an equally roomy tool box, that has plenty of space for additional items that you may wish to place within it. On your journey, you may wish to craft additional items that you can call upon when the time is right, it's your mind remember. Next time you feel the ominous dark clouds approaching on the horizon try to arm yourself and face the threat with optimism and might.

Use the new skills and methods you have absorbed; how do they make you feel?

Note down and record your wins, however small, additionally record down the losses and examine what could be done differently next time, never sit still in your mind.

Normal service will not be resumed

Change will take place and others around you may not always like it, as you will not be a carpet anymore, you will no longer let people or feelings walk over you unabated. You will be a stronger independent individual that is aware of your own needs and wishes. This may be difficult for some of your acquaintances to understand, as it will essentially be a new you, hopefully they will soon realise that this development is better for everyone but most importantly, you.

You will challenge uncomfortable feelings and situations, remembering that you and your spirits are the priority in everything that you undertake. The timeframe for all of this is not an issue as it is not a race, better to have these new skills and approaches as second nature over a longer term, than falling over on day one.

It could be the case that when you are feeling strong enough that you can also include additional good feeling activities, such as doing some voluntary work in your local area. This will allow you to mix in a new group of acquaintances that may have similar interests as you. The face to face sharing of experiences is so important for us and it also cultivates our confidence and self-esteem.

The future

I leave you now, hoping that you are better equipped to deal with your depression but be cautious as it takes a long time to subdue a Boris. It has been a part of your life for potentially a long time and change will take a while, do not rush it.

This will be an on-going battle as you continue in your individual growth and development. If you experience setbacks then use them to learn from, so that next time you are better prepared. Try to be realistic in your expectations on your own growth and rein in excessive changes to stay within your capabilities. Consider it as a runner doing a marathon; a regular pace wins over just speed.

The future is what you want it to be, as the ability to change is within all of us and correctly applied your future is within your terms for once.

Always check back to this guide when you need reminders to assist you during difficult times. Also, there is plenty of up to date information available on the Internet from lots of organisations, some also have online forums and chat rooms that can be a place to share experiences in a less public way.
I will give a few of the most prominent and well known ones:

- http://www.mind.org.uk
- http://www.rethink.org
- https://www.samaritans.org

- https://www.studentsagainstdepression.org
- http://www.sane.org

Remember, scan through your local papers, flyers and notice boards to see if there are local support groups close by.

Finally; always be vigilant and feel your emotions, taking corrective action if you are overdoing it or if it just does not feel right.

I wish you the very best for your future.

Banish Boris to the under stairs cupboard!!

Printed in Poland
by Amazon Fulfillment
Poland Sp. z o.o., Wrocław